New Japan

The economic renaissance -- and its enemies

Akira Kawamoto

Akira Kawamoto retired in 2012 from Japan's Ministry of Economy, Trade and Industry, following a 31-year career in which he served as the director of numerous divisions (including of the electricity market during the reformist era of Prime Minister Koizumi), and worked at the OECD in Paris. He is currently a senior partner at Aspirant Group, a private equity fund in Tokyo, and project professor in the Economics Department at Keio University. Mr. Kawamoto is also a member of the Japanese Government's Regulatory Reform Commission working-group on business, start-ups and IT, which advises the prime minister on policy matters. He is the author of two books in Japanese: "Why Japan Cannot Follow Through With Reform" (Nikkei Publishing, 2013) and "Regulatory Reform" (1998).

1

Acknowledgments

I am honored to present this ebook to English readers, a condensed version of a book I published in 2013 in Japanese, "Why Japan Cannot Follow Through With Reform" (Nikkei Publishing). I am grateful to my friends, family and colleagues (past and present) who encouraged me to present my views publicly. Also, I express my sincere thanks to Kenneth Cukier, The Economist's Data Editor and formerly the paper's Tokyo correspondent in 2007-12, for his generous assistance. Without his warm encouragement and excellent editing, this work would have never have come to exist.

Akira Kawamoto

Tokyo, June 2014

Chapter 1.   Is Japan back?

The Reawakening

The challenge facing Japan is not what to do, but whether the country's leaders have the muscle to act. Decades of insidious incentives and misguided policy mechanisms throughout industry and government have paralyzed the possibility of reforming the archaic practices that hold the country back. Yet there are reasons for optimism: leaders in politics, business and the bureaucracy -- as well as the public -- see the need to reform institutions and practices that fail to serve the long-term interests of the country. A failure to fully make the needed changes will plunge Japan back into the miasma of economic malaise from which it is now emerging.

By all accounts, Japan's 20-year suffering seems to be coming to an end. Since Prime Minister Shinzo Abe took office at the end of 2012, the Japanese economy has continued to improve.

Signs of a revival have produced a sunny mood in a nation troubled with self-doubt, notably after ceding its position to China as the world's second-largest economy.

Following the leadership of Junichiro Koizumi, an exceptionally charismatic politician who led Japan for six years and left office in 2006, six prime ministers (including Mr. Abe himself), all found it difficult to stay in office for more than a year. The disappointment only deepened during the administrations of the Democratic Party of Japan, which was initially hailed in 2009 as people's liberator from the long and increasingly mediocre reign of the LDP.

Mr. Abe's policies have impressed international investors. Japanese share prices rose by around 60% at the outset of his administration, as investors sought to increase their holdings of Japanese companies in their portfolios. The prime minister's team seems to be adept at wooing foreign audiences, especially compared to past administrations. Mr. Abe declared that "Japan is back" when he visited the United States in February 2013, when he trumpeted his economic policy of "Abenomics". It comprises so-called "three arrows": a punchier monetary policy, more stimulus spending, and reforms to unwind decades of special-interest policies that have strangled Japan but are politically hard to undo.

As the world economy recovers from the financial crisis, investors are scouring the world looking at risks and opportunities. Japan actually looks pretty good. America's slow recovery, uncertainty in the euro zone, and questions about Chinese growth are topics of the day. That the Japanese economy has made it back onto the world's radar screens was unimaginable just a few years ago. The issue is pertinent for the global economy. What happens in Japan has far-reaching implications for businesses worldwide, from the machines and process-technologies that other firms use to produce their goods, to the finished products that consumers buy. This actually remained true for decades, though since the downturn of the 1990s it received little notice. Just as importantly, an economically robust Japan also serves its own national interests. The country needs to stabilize its social spending, which is swelling due to a quickly aging society, to name just one pressing concern. Having the financial means to provide a bright future for its youth is obviously another.

This highlights the fact that the most controversial and most difficult part of Abenomics -- the "Third Arrow" of structural reform -- will increasingly be scrutinized worldwide as a proxy for Japan's commitment to change. It is said that the Abe administration is very sensitive to "market voices" and that this sensitivity has established confidence in its economic policies so far. Yet it also means that Abenomics will be judged at a higher standard among the international community of investors and policy makers.

International scrutiny

It is for that reason that I pen this essay, an English summary of a book I published last year in Japanese called "Why Japan Cannot Follow Through With Reform" (Nikkei Publishing, 2013). I left the Japanese government in 2012 after spending more than 30 years in various economic policy functions. I also had a chance to work at the OECD Secretariat on the regulatory reform project between 1995 and 1999. The book published last year was based on my experiences at the heart of the Japanese system of governance and industry.

I argued that Japan's economic policy agenda is pretty well established, thanks to years of debate among numerous experts during Japan's two "lost decades". The most important issue for Japan now is not what to do but how to do it ·· and how to do it in an effective and timely way. It is crucial to identify the reasons that have prevented past reform efforts from taking hold. Unwinding these obsolete features of Japan will be critical for the country's future, for which I offer my analysis and recommendations in the pages that follow.

When I started my career in Japanese officialdom in the beginning of 1980s, the world was enthralled with decoding the secrets of Japan's success. The United States, worried about its booming trade deficit with Japan, minted many experts on Japan's systems of politics, economy, society and technology.

Some 30 years later, it is harder for people to judge where Japan is headed. Since the downturn in the 1990s, the intellectual links between Japan and the rest of the world have steadily declined. People have fewer resources to help them understand the structure of Japanese politics and economy. This is why I am spurred to bring my voice to the conversation, and where I hope to make a contribution.

The first arrow: monetary policy blitzkrieg

Mr. Abe's team has made its economic policy thinking unusually transparent. They formulated the scheme based on the tale of "Three Arrows", when the Great Warlord Motonari Mouri in the 16th century is said to have shown his three siblings that even if they can break arrows one by one, three arrows together cannot be broken. Fittingly, Mr. Abe's family came from the homeland of the House of Mouri.

The first arrow of Abenomics is aggressive monetary policy. When the LDP was not in power and before Mr. Abe was elected the president of the party, he accepted the main position of a policy group aiming to defeat Japan's deflation by arguing against the Bank of Japan's (BOJ) actions.

Reflecting his strong commitment to a more muscular monetary policy, Mr. Abe consistently called for the appointment of a new BOJ governor. As prime minister, he arranged Haruhiko Kuroda, a former vice minister of finance and later the head of the Asian Development Bank, to replace Masaaki Shirakawa. Mr. Kuroda was well known for his views that Japan's economy could improve if the BOJ were to change its traditionally conservative stance. Since taking office in March 2013, the new governor repaid the trust by the prime minister by pushing the BOJ to commit to inflation targeting and to an aggressive expansion of monetary policy.

While the majority of economic experts in Japanese academia and think tanks are not fully persuaded by the logic of the new monetary initiative, it has largely worked as hoped. It was Abe's Blitzkrieg: surprisingly quick and packing massive force. Assets prices of equities and property have risen and the yen has depreciated against major currencies, supporting an upward shift of economic indicators like consumption and exports. Prices are also showing clear signs of rising.

Of course it is one thing that the signs are moving in the right direction and another that the degree of movement is sufficient. It can be argued (and frequently is argued) that monetary policy alone is not enough to revive the Japanese economy.

The second arrow: dubious public spending

The shooting of the first arrow caught people by surprise and produced results, at least so far. The second arrow, fiscal expansion, on the other hand is more questionable.

Shortly after taking office, the Abe cabinet approved a supplementary budget for fiscal year 2012 ending in March 2013 that expanded government spending by ¥13.1 trillion (roughly $130 billion). In general, public spending -- even if it means deeper budget deficits and more debt -- helps an economy during a downturn. However, Japan's fiscal condition is already the worst among major industrial countries.

This is due to many factors. First, successive administrations spent lavishly on public works, which although justified by Keynesian economics, was actually motivated by political favoritism. Second, more public expenditure for social security is required because of an aging population. Third, Japan suffered stagnant tax revenue due to weak income growth and a failure to raise taxes (the current consumption tax rate of 8% was only increased from 5% in April 2014 after years of handwringing).

The Diet passed a second supplementary budget in February 2014, adding another ¥5.5 trillion in public spending. The major reason was to address the economic headwinds caused by the rise in the consumption tax. Experts generally welcomed the tax increase, and fiscal conditions are expected to improve substantially, largely because of more tax revenue. But concerns remain as to whether the improvement can be sustained.

Reliance on public works to sustain growth has to be reduced at some point in the near future. There must be social security reform to reign in long-term outlays, such as putting off pension entitlement age or more private funding to healthcare. And perhaps most importantly, Japan's business sector must play a more vigorous role in leading economic growth.

The third arrow: structural reform

This lays the groundwork for the third arrow, the growth strategy. As legend goes, just two arrows alone are likely to be too weak to hold. The third arrow is an indispensable element in Abenomics. As there are now relatively few things that one can do about the first two arrows already shot, attention naturally shifts to the third.

The first two arrows are concerned with macroeconomics and its actors are clearly identified as central bankers and government fiscal authorities. The third arrow, by contrast, concerns itself with microeconomics: various types of market failures and policy recommendations to make businesses and households more eager to invest or consume. The actors of the third arrow are much more numerous and diverse, hence the growth policies cover a whole universe of government activities. (Though to be sure, there are limits on government policies to influence private sector actions.) All this means that fostering growth should be a government-wide project. It requires sustained and concerted efforts among various government branches, supervised closely by the center. It should be also based on sound microeconomics insights.

Since the Japanese economy started its gradual decline after the bubble burst in the early 1990s, policymakers and experts have repeated analyses of the causes of stagnation and asked about ways of solving them. Some issues have already been successfully addressed (such as bad debt problems), and others worsened (like public debt) while still some others are being tried (aggressive monetary easing). But in the area of growth policies, the continual discussions among economic experts for over two decades have produced a broad convergence of views. They include:

- Regulatory reform to expand areas for business activities: various government regulations are outdated and prevent expansion of business activities. In some areas like professional services, energy and transportation, there has been even a retreat from earlier reforms. In other heavily regulated sectors such as agriculture and healthcare, reforms have been nominal at the best.

- Market opening: though trade barriers have been substantially reduced in the manufacturing sector, the areas of agriculture and some services remain closed to foreign access.

- Incentives for firms to shift resources from inefficient and stagnant areas to efficient and growing ones:

  ➢ Rigid labor rules covering life-long employment should be relaxed; policies should encourage women to play a more substantial role in the workforce

  ➢ More effective corporate governance is needed to motivate management to improve profitability through responsible yet aggressive risk-taking

- Public investment in education, science, technology and innovation: more choices for education are needed; foster more venture capital investment through policies aimed at "cloning" Silicon Valley.

Foreign observers tend to focus on several big issues, such as the low rate of women's labor participation, the corporate tax rate or immigration. These are of course badly needed. But the discussion must be put in the context of a more comprehensive range of reforms -- and an aggressive timetable to achieve them.

The failure of past reform efforts

Experts' views may differ on the relative importance of a given policy and which should take priority. They may disagree on specific policy measures. But there can be no debate on the areas of reform themselves. The economic policy agenda for Japan has already been made clear before policymakers.

Following the Koizumi administration, each of the short-lived prime ministers (a year in office was the norm between 2006 and 2012) produced his own "growth strategy". So there have been numerous strategies, now completely forgotten. Making strategy became routine to the government officials. On each occasion, the main title of the strategy and emphasis was a little different, according to the preferences of the politicians in power. But the policies they put forward were largely the same.

Yet a problems is that the substance of the reforms are always compromised, as is the speed and clarity, because of fierce resistance from politicians and the bureaucracy, supported by special interests. As a result, no fundamental changes were implemented, further hobbled because of the short lifespans of the administrations. So the reality of Japan's growth strategy drama is that numerous documents were produced -- making a generous financial contribution to the paper and printing industries, but little real progress overall. Often, political leaders deflect debate by convening a "vision group" consisting of big names -- authoritative professors or respected business leaders -- who discuss the future in general terms, but don't strike to the core of the special interests that hold Japan back.

However, this must end. It is now time to think deeper. Rather than talk in circles about what to do, we must tackle the problems of the mechanisms and incentives in Japan's politics and bureaucracy.

Chapter 2. Struggling to bounce back

What prevents reform

The area covered by the third arrow of Abenomics, the growth-enhancing microeconomic reforms, is vast. It involves many dimensions that require strong and persistent political leadership in order to plan and implement the measures.

A typical example is regulatory reform. In many instances, regulations actively work against new entrants in an industry. Incumbents lobby to retain the status quo to maintain their profits, their economic rents. Economic analyses show that regulatory reform increases public welfare by lower prices and producing more output, hence the benefits are dispersed broadly among many consumers. The social rents that reform takes away, on the other hand, is concentrated on just a few firms. So they have a burning interest in keeping their perks.

Consider the electricity sector. Ten utilities have enjoyed a virtual regional monopoly for more than half a century. Regulatory reform aims to introduce competition in the industry. Electricity users, such as firms and households, who have suffered from expensive bills can save money. Though such saving is only a small percentage of their incomes, in aggregate the gains to the overall economy are huge. However, this would make life for the electricity industry poorer, more uncertain and riskier. So they fight tooth-and-nail to keep their privileges and excessive profits. For the public, reform is not a subject of life or death, while for power-industry people, it is.

The politics of special interests

In this situation, the politicians -- the final arbitrators of regulations -- are under constant pressures from special-interest groups such as Federation of Electric Power Companies in Japan, while the general public, the diverse recipients of potential benefits of reform, find it difficult to organize itself and make its voice heard.

However they do have a chance to influence politicians' actions at the polling stations. If the choice is clearly presented to them, reform is good reason for voters to support a politician or political party. Mr. Koizumi succeeded in winning elections easily under reform platforms three times in office. The DPJ, seen as being free from special interests and thus capable in pushing through reforms, won a landslide victory in the 2009 general election. It began its time in power with higher public support ratings even than that given to Mr. Koizumi.

The snag is that elections are normally held once every several years. Between them, lobbying groups are more visible and seem to have the upper hand. So the challenge is, how can political leaders guide, cajole or negotiate with fellow politicians towards reform?

1. The political dimension of reform

Government as a federation of ministries

The politics of special interests is a universal problem for democracy, not unique to Japan. But the country's governance structure adds further difficulties that hold back reform.

In modern society, government must be supported by a civil service. Yet it is also well known that in areas like budgets and regulatory reform, bureaucrats responsible for specific areas such as transportation, agriculture, education or communication, tend to resist central control for efficiency and reform. Instead, they seek to keep their autonomy.

The tendency to remain autonomous is more prominent in Japan than other countries. Life-long employment is still the norm, and is at its paragon in the national bureaucracy. It is your personal feeling that when you become an official after all the relevant procedures, you have been hired by the ministry, not by the government. Such feelings are reaffirmed by the experiences in your career.

Your position is totally controlled by the ministry's formidable personnel department. And as anyone who has experienced life in Japanese officialdom knows, what position you get gives you the strongest incentives in work. The personnel department is directly answerable to the ministry's administrative vice minister, the top bureaucrat in each ministry. As such, it commands the fiercest loyalty of thousands of men and women working in the ministry.

The Japanese government is virtually a federation of powerful ministries, rather than one unified entity. Each ministry of Japan resembles one large-scale corporation. Its leverage over an individual official is strong because you will be taken care of by the ministry even after you retire from government service -- and from your earliest days, you know it.

The iron triangle

That means the Ministry has control over many positions outside the government, albeit informally. So the Ministry has an organizational impetus to keep and to expand its sphere of influence, which may not always be consistent with the public interest. For example, the ministry may have an excessive desire to maintain public corporations, with influence over the appointment of many posts, even though these organizations may no longer be necessary.

The interaction among of politicians, bureaucrats and industry is called the "iron triangle". The three groups, notably the regulatory agencies and the regulated industries cooperate with each other to defend the status quo. Japan has arguably the strongest such triangular structure in the world.

Previous reforms introduced measures to mitigate this unhealthy cooperation, such as improving transparency by publishing the deliberation sessions of policy councils, and creating a mandatory public-comment process for regulatory proposals. But in terms of the overall incentives for government officials, the situation is unchanged. It is difficult to fully mobilize officials' energy and resources for regulatory reform, in order to provide politicians with analysis and advice, or to persuade industry of the need for change.

Leadership above, setbacks on the ground

It is commendable that the Abe administration has recognized the importance of political leadership for reform. Leaders at the top have repeated to claim that regulatory reform is major challenge for their growth strategies. Indeed, raising visibility of an economic policy agenda by alluding to the popular fable of "The Tale of Three Arrows" is in itself a victory in political communication.

Yet this success invites more scrutiny. Since the start of the Abe cabinet, the Regulatory

Reform Commission (RRC), a group of independent experts commissioned to make recommendations to the cabinet, has been reactivated and produced a number of successes. Though the impact of each is relatively small, together they signify progress. However, ministries with various regulatory powers have been able to skirt control from the center. Take labor regulations, for example. Although firms' ability to use "dispatched" (that is, outside-contractor) workers was reduced by legislation during the DPJ government in 2009-12, even further restrictions have since been put in place, in the form of mandatory employment of workers up to pension-entitlement age.

Where once policies were directed towards more entry such as the taxi industry or legal services, there has since been a reversal under the watch of LDP government. In the agriculture sector, the government plans to revise a policy of reducing rice acreage. This was a welcomed change by some. But experts like Kazuhito Yamashita, the former Director General in the Ministry of

Agriculture, Forestry and Fisheries (MAFF), and now a research director at the Canon Institute for Global Studies, criticize new policy, arguing that it will merely shift production from staple rice to feed rice (with the result that production of staple rice is still restricted and its price kept high). It is anything but a fundamental reform.

Whether large-scale, efficient producers may expand is unclear. Ownership of farmland is heavily restricted in Japan. Recently, when the government proposed a bill to encourage the transfer of farmland to able and willing producers, lawmakers in the agricultural committee of the Diet made changes so that the transfer happened under the control of the local agricultural community. These communities, often led by conservative cooperatives, do not welcome new entrants. Although the original intention of the reform bill was good, the final outcome makes it difficult for new agri-businesses to start, typically by younger people. This in the end hurts Japanese agriculture, whose farmers are rapidly aging, but such is the way policies are made.

The political governance of reform

There is a governance problem in the Japanese cabinet system, as Professor Naoto Nonaka, a political scientist at Gakushuin University, points out in his widely-read book on Japanese politics in 2013. Cabinet meetings offer little substantial discussion, and ministers behave largely as representative of each portfolio bureaucracy. So the forum cannot function as rallying point for political leadership.

To address this, Japan should devise a new mechanism to hold substantial discussions among ministers, similar to the "cabinet committee" systems adopted by Britain and France, says Professor Nonaka. Without such a system, it will be difficult for politicians in ministerial positions to overcome the built-in resistance from the bureaucracy on controversial issues such as regulatory reform or budgetary control. Even if the prime minister's office puts forward a reform policy, the vital on-the-ground implementation at lower levels of the bureaucracy and with local regulatory rules, etc, must be closely monitored, to ensure that the policy is not undermined.

One good sign about the Abe administration is that in its first 18 months in power since its inauguration at the end of 2012, there had been no cabinet reshuffles. Having the same politician as minister for several years is a necessary starting point for effective oversight. However, the Abe Cabinet in this regard is very much the exception to Japan's bad habit of rotating ministerial portfolios frequently among politicians in the ruling party as reward, not as an appointment based on merit. And obviously one cannot remain satisfied with this very basic level achievement, but demand that more be done.

The management tools of politics

Building an effective cabinet system is not the only

political challenge for reform. If a ruling party obtains a mandate for reform in an election, its leaders' job to follow through in the subsequent administration will be relatively easy. But this is not always the case in Japan, as was seen in the Upper House election in July 2013.

Political leaders in democracies usually have some tools at their disposal to force through reform measures; they can resort to party discipline like in Germany, or parliamentary rules to allow the government to decide on the legislative schedule like in France or Britain. Unfortunately, Japan lacks these instruments of the effective use of political power, noted Mr. Nonaka.

Furthermore, there is a question of the disparity of voting power between urban and rural areas. The countryside has been consistently overrepresented in the Diet. Numerous Supreme Court rulings have raised the unconstitutionality of these elections (though stopping short of nullifying the vote). Despite this, the Diet has been reluctant to make the fundamental changes to rectify the problem.

2. The bureaucracy and reform

Loyalty as asset

Having the political will to reform and provide effective leadership is an indispensable first step. But the crucial second step is follow-through. A reform agenda requires that the bureaucracy effectively support the political will. And this poses difficulties.

Every year, the Japanese government recruits hundreds of the ablest university students in the country. They are eager to work for the public good and their loyalty to their respective ministries cannot be doubted. But the problem is that under the current structure and governance system of the "iron triangle," their talents and vigor are mostly poorly used.

Each Japanese ministry is a largely autonomous organization run by permanent staff

31

officials. Political supervision has been traditionally sporadic and weak: only several politicians are appointed to a given ministry with thousands of permanent staff who spend their entire careers there. Officials are moved among various positions in the ministry every two or three years, a rotation strictly based on seniority measured by entry year. Through such personnel control from the center, the ministry can effectively influence the actions of officials.

This sort of structure has the advantage of obtaining the fierce loyalty of the officials. It is commonplace in Kasumigaseki, the district in downtown Tokyo teeming with ministries' buildings, that officials work through the night, sleepless, to prepare large reams of papers to brief their ministers early the next morning, who answer questions at Diet sessions.

Deviating from the public good

Yet the ideal of public service can be seriously

compromised if such loyalty is directed towards maintaining the iron triangle structure. Ministry officials in particular can closely ally themselves with politicians in respective areas, helping such political "tribes" to circumvent attempts at reform. MAFF officials, for example, closely work with Diet members on the agriculture committee to modify proposed reform bills.

Another example is fiscal policy. Government spending is the second arrow of Abenomics, even though Japan's public debt dwarfs other industrialized nations. Despite raising the consumption tax rate in April 2014, the debt is forecast to balloon. Japan needs not only to increase tax revenue, but also to control spending, argues Professor Hideaki Tanaka, of the Graduate School of Global Governance at Meiji University and a former official at the Ministry of Finance (MOF), in his 2013 book on Japan's public finances.

Based on an exhaustive study of international examples, he points out that the control of public spending can be greatly improved by introducing more transparency in budgetary decisions. Also, it can be improved by creating a legal framework that political leaders can use to limit their fellow politicians' relentless pressure for more spending. Professor Tanaka offers a number of good practices from Europe and North America, such as using more objective economic forecasts during budget talks, eliminating loopholes in spending-request rules, or more adopting binding policy-impact analyses.

One wonders why MOF, the cream of the Japanese bureaucracy, has been very slow to embrace these ideas. If adopted, they will help achieve MOF's prime goal as a public body, namely, to control spending and improve fiscal conditions. MOF can even become popular, seen by the public as fighting special interests' reckless pressure. The answer, Mr. Tanaka suggests, is that MOF prefers to play the role of backroom political arbitrator than to become the official champion of fiscal discipline.

The bureaucracy as political player

Why should the MOF refuse to play such a natural role, which is clearly within its remit? In Japan, voters have feared an overly powerful bureaucracy following several scandals in 1990s that shocked the public. The ministries' attempts to expand their spheres of influence by securing outside jobs for former officials are under constant scrutiny. From time to time, the politicians are called upon to rein it in.

By keeping political power, the bureaucrats retain a bit of latitude to cut a deal with politicians on these matters when necessary. Reform may end up putting officials in a highly contentious position against powerful industry lobbies. At the same time, many politicians are eager to pressure the ministry to water down reform measures. The ministry, as a savvy political operator, wants to minimize its political risks. So it discourages officials from pursuing vigorous reforms that might expose the ministry to controversy.

This was certainly the case in previous reform attempts. After introducing several significant steps to open up the electricity market in 2003, the Ministry of Economy, Trade and Industry (METI) gradually relented to political pressures and stopped using its regulatory powers to open up utilities' transmission networks. The ability for new firms to enter the market was severely curtailed. Ultimately, the prospect of full liberalization of the market, at one time a certainty, was indefinitely postponed. It was a disappointing setback for officials (such as myself) who were engaged in the reform legislation -- as well as a setback for the Japan people, who were forced to pay excessive prices.

Three years after the crisis at the Fukushima Daiichi nuclear power plant in 2011, METI has begun to renew its reform efforts. The big utility firm had lost so much social standing that it was hard for them to fight the bills that aimed to restructure the energy market and unwind archaic policies that protect incumbent energy operators. Creating workable, liberalized electricity market from the existing, highly-monopolized industry requires constant vigilance for substantial length of time. Whether such efforts are fully implemented this time will depend on the reform of the bureaucracy itself.

A missing force for reform

The role of the civil service, in contrast to that of elected politicians, is to offer useful expertise for society. Its members should be recruited, evaluated and promoted on that basis. Such a system is called a meritocracy and the model official is the technocrat. Ideally, permanent officials should present information and policy choices based on accurate and objective analysis, even if those options are politically unfavorable. However, such officials may not be liked nor evaluated highly by their political masters.

If politicians have control over

bureaucrats' promotions, then the civil servants are likely to avoid pursuing necessary but controversial policies, notably curtailing budgets or fundamental regulatory reform. In Japan, legally, ministers have few restrictions on the appointments of senior officials. Politicians traditionally have not intervened in most cases. Things seemed to change when DPJ came to power in 2009, claiming they had the power to replace senior officials at will. As it happens, such upheavals did not take place much in practice. But it highlighted the vulnerability that the bureaucracy faces.

The impact of this on the minds of government officials has been substantial, leading to a "minimum political risk strategy" that lingers on. The result is a passive and static bureaucracy, making it difficult to find the driving force for substantial reform that the economy requires.

Benchmarks for civil service reform

To be sure, a competent and far-sighted minister can deal with these problems, and can encourage and work with subordinate officials to enact necessary reforms. It is possible that such an individual could emerge -- but it may be impractical to hope too much for such a political leader to step forward. At the same time, for the bureaucracy, safeguarding itself from the whims of politicians serves their self-interests too, because a change of ruling parties will continue to take place. In order for Japan to follow through with reform, it is necessary to mobilize the bureaucracy's talent and energy. This requires changes in the civil service's personnel system.

Based on my observations following more than thirty years in government service, three important points stand out as benchmarks for reform:

1) Break ministerial silos and reward collaboration

The most serious defect of the bureaucracy is

its vertical segmentation by self-serving ministries. That results in a severe lack of coordination among different sections leading to indecision. Yes, "turf wars" are universal. But within Japan's system of governance, it is elevated into an art form. It has been recommended many times that a government "control tower," such as the cabinet office, should be given more responsibility. But it is the last thing that the ministries would submit to. The fundamental reason is that each ministry is run like an independent corporation; it sees no interest in rewarding officials to work with other ministries for the public good.

2) Introduce standardized processes of evaluation and external review

After being left to the autonomy of ministry officials, the civil service personnel system is poorly organized, with informal processes and little accountability. There is virtually no possibility of external input, except for in rare cases of political intervention. Instead, a clearly defined system involving a committee that includes independent outsiders should be convened, at least for senior appointments. A sense of fairness in promotions will encourage officials to genuinely serve the public good.

3) Increase openness of selection

If one follows the principles of a meritocracy, then talents should be sought beyond the boundaries of any particular ministry. But Japanese ministries prefer internal candidates based on order and submission, not notice and application. It leads to generation after generation of insiders who have shown they won't rock the boat, rather than creative outsiders with a transformational vision. As a remedy, an open application process or more clearly defined procedure of vetting candidates without a bias for insiders should be adopted. This will energize officials and invigorate individuals' talents for producing results.

The good news is that the Abe government has moved forward in these areas. The Diet is passing the Civil Service Reform Act, which establishes a more centralized personnel system for senior officials in all ministries. The rules also strengthen the powers of the ministers' offices, to help them to lead the process.

These modest reforms address the first of the three recommendations: they contribute to a better functioning government by motivating officials to work effectively. But unless the system deals with the second and third points (on process and openness), the danger of political favoritism remains. The prime minister's office or individual ministers might only promote officials who provide advice they like to hear. How the government will use a new personnel system is untested; the "management capacity" of governing politicians and administrators remains an open question.

Chapter 3. Business bounces back: corporate reform

Government policies play an important role in spurring economic growth. For example the state can change regulatory rules, invest in scientific research, develop human capital, and negotiate with other governments for more liberal trade and investment regimes. In the preceding pages, I have described how Japanese politicians and bureaucrats must do more to implement these sorts of necessary reforms, even if they meet resistance from vested interests.

Yet such recommendations assume that once government implements the right policies, the corporate sector will respond: expand production, increase investment and create jobs. At this point, we should be careful not to overestimate the impact of government policy on the overall economy. The share of heavily regulated industries such as health care, electricity and agriculture in the Japanese economy is relatively small. Vast

43

areas of manufacturing and services are left largely to the private sector, with less state influence.

Still, government matters a lot. Regulations covering the labor market or financial markets have huge impact. The government's ambition to enact reforms affects business and household expectations, which in turn influences investment and consumption. That said, in Japan another issue is whether, after government implements the right policies, the business sector can respond vigorously enough to re-ignite growth. Japanese companies still have a lot of internal reorganization and restructuring to do. Their potential may not fully materialize due to the rigidity of their organization, processes and practices -- or because of simple inertia.

Low corporate profitability

One of the most notable aspects of Japanese businesses is their consistently low level of profitability compared with their international peers. When a firm's average profits over time do not improve, three market forces should induce changes in the way the company carries out its business: competitive threats, financial pressure and shareholder pressure. But in Japan, these forces are not strong enough to influence management behavior. Consider each one individually:

1) Market competition

Firms that that have low profit levels (or are unprofitable) are unable to invest as much as they might wish, and are likely to be less competitive, in term of pricing power and product quality. Customers will find their products less attractive. Their market share will be squeezed and ultimately the firms will be driven out of the market. However, many Japanese firms today have secured substantial position in the domestic market, which is still large. Although industries such as electronics have experienced a tough business environment in recent years, many others have not feel challenged with survival -- unlike US firms, which often feel threatened by fast-growing upstarts, or European firms that are exposed to international competition.

2) Financial pressure

Firms posting low profitability will increasingly be seen by lenders such as banks as more likely to experience repayment difficulties and to potentially default. Lenders will monitor firms more closely and may insist on fundamental changes to the business strategy or management. In the past, Japanese banks had substantial leverage over the firms, because of the heavy reliance on bank lending. (This obviously brought its own set of troubles, as the banking crisis of the 1990s made clear.) But now -- partially in reaction to this history -- many firms are sitting on large cash reserve and do not heed banks' advice easily. In addition, Japanese banks themselves are not under pressure to achieve a high level of profitability, and hence they tend to avoid confrontations with borrowers, particularly big ones.

3) Shareholders' pressure

The stock prices of less profitable firms tend to fall, and they find it harder to finance investment. Institutional investors may request changes. With meager prospects, various investment funds may approach the firms or their shareholders, either to obtain a stake, full control or to recommend divesting certain business divisions. Yet most Japanese companies are run by managers with lifetime employment, and hence are deeply suspicious of "outsiders" like investment funds. Moreover, the Japanese business community is rather homogeneous. The managers of big institutional investors such as insurance firms and trust banks, share a common background with their peers in the corporate world, and resist confronting the underperforming firms. Many continue the practice of cross-shareholding and cross-appointment of board directors, which stifles dissent. And many have adopted defensive measures against takeovers, which remove the pressure to improve corporate performance.

This has neutered the ambition and drive of Japan businesses, resulting in a lack of focus, speed, agility, vision, and produced an excessive aversion to risks. It has also led to deficient governance among Japanese companies, even if they possess superior technologies, employee loyalty, a solid customer base and excellent brands. For growth to accelerate, progress on these three fronts is needed, along with government reforms.

Animal spirits and Abenomics

Many Japanese companies originated from technology start-ups established by innovative and ambitious engineers. Think of Akio Mori at Sony and Konosuke Matsushita at Panasonic, to name just two. Over time, the "animal spirits" of the founders have been lost in the bureaucratic organization of the many giant firms that dot Japan's business landscape. The issue is whether such spirits can be revived. For example, managers' incentives to take more risks can be enhanced by effective corporate governance, rewarding well-considered risk-taking and punishing both recklessness and indecision.

On the question of revitalizing the animal spirits of business managers, Abenomics may have had a positive impact. First, when general prices rise, price differentials will become wider than when under deflation. During periods of inflation, some prices rise more quickly than others. That creates opportunities for arbitrage, as well as more business risks, and offers investment opportunities (as well as possibilities that the competence of managers are revealed more clearly and quickly).

Secondly, prices tend to rise faster than wages. As a result, real wages may decline, and firms find it more profitable to increase output and employment. Although this development may perplex the Abe administration, which urges wage increases to encourage consumption (one would think they should rather welcome the decline of real wages!), the favorable business climate may encourage managers to take bolder actions that have an even bigger payback to the economy.

On the other hand, it may be the case that Japanese firms have been accustomed to low expectations for so long, and many of its managers do not feel pressed to act as assertively and rapidly as faster economic growth demands. Tellingly, a Cabinet Office survey found that the deeper the recession, the more US firms tended to anticipate higher future growth, while Japanese firms were more likely to expect lower growth. For Japanese firms' animal spirits to revive, Abenomics may not be sufficient. Much more needs to happen on the corporate side.

Change the definition of competition

What needs to happen in Japanese business to

revitalize the economy? The usual complaint of industrialists goes like this: "The competition is too hard. There are just too many firms in the domestic market, and our narrow industry, but we cannot do anything other than attack each other until the end!" And then they let out a long, defeatist sigh. To be sure, the refrain has some truth to it. But it has been uttered for so long and in so many contexts, that one can only wonder why the situation still exists!

A reasonable answer is that firms have established certain market positions and have found ways to cope, particularly in terms of low profitability. Continual price competition in homogeneous markets is the norm. After all, overcapacity is hard to maintain for a long period of time. Traditional Japanese companies are inhabited by people with similar educational and social backgrounds, and similar thinking. Just consider those in manufacturing, notably steel, chemicals, machinery, electronics and automobiles. Certainly fierce rivalries exist. But it usually ends in a war of attrition. Firms are run by "salarymen" (and almost only men, rarely women) who enjoy employment for life; their strategies are closely watched by others and quickly copied.

Rather than focusing on the most promising and profitable activities, Japanese companies tend to keep many unprofitable, underperforming businesses. And old rivalries often persist even when many in the sector admit that head-on competition with similar products is not futile, and that consolidation is the most rational course. It is necessary to change the mindset of business leaders, to shift their benchmark of what competition means, from one that is aimed at the domestic market and relatively static, to one that is global and dynamic. It means overcoming narrow-minded rivalries and searching out unique business opportunities and innovations with an eye to global competitiveness.

Some Japanese manufactures have started to move in this direction. For instance, the old archrivals Hitachi and Mitsubishi Heavy

Industries have combined their industrial machinery businesses, such as steel-making machines and thermal power system. Yet in another case, similar consolidation talks between two large ship makers failed, due to an internal resistance to join forces. Much more consolidation should follow by many firms -- and fast.

The key element of this change is an open mindedness among management. Because Japanese firms' management teams are uniquely homogeneous, the change in mindset requires someone at board meetings to break ranks and say: "Hey! Things are no longer sustainable. Let's look at the situation afresh, without prejudice!" In Japan's corporate culture, this is exceedingly hard to do. After all, the managers probably attained their positions precisely because they do not speak out.

At the same time, cross shareholdings among blue-chip companies, most of whose headquarters are within a few kilometers of each other in central Tokyo, still remain (though has declined substantially from their heyday). This often hampers effective corporate governance. As just one example of old Japan's reluctance to change, Keidanren, the most powerful and traditional business lobby, refuses to endorse a proposal for mandatory independent board directors for public companies.

Make banks more assertive

Japanese banks have lost most of their influence over big corporations, as we've discussed above. But when the persistent, low profitability of some firms led to financial troubles -- as in recent cases in the electronics industry -- companies ultimately found they needed to rely on banks. Some bankers in Japan know that the banks should have acted earlier. Banks themselves may benefit from revisiting their relationships with big firms. The companies, when performance is stagnant, may be more easily persuaded to rethink and recalibrate their business strategies, before real troubles hit.

For mid- and small-size firms, banks still maintain their clout. But here, the banking industry itself has a problem of overcapacity. Because there are too many banks, smaller firms usually have access to many willing lenders. As a result, interest rates are depressed and do not reflect the actual risk of the borrowers. And the near-zero policy rate set by the Bank of Japan, the spearhead of the current super-lax monetary policy that is Abenomics' First Arrow, does little to help in this regard.

If banks start to charge interest rates according to the real risk associated with borrowers in line with the practices of other industrialized countries, Japan's business sector would be more sensitive to corporate profitability. Decisions whether to invest or disinvest would be swifter, leading to faster growth. The Financial Services Agency (FSA), the country's banking regulator, can help by highlighting the importance of asset quality in bank supervision. Once this sort of policy is enacted, the financing of riskier businesses by investment funds would likely expand.

Politicians, on the other hand, should refrain from interfering with bank lending, such as demanding that banks agree to a moratorium on loan repayments by small and medium sized borrowers during recessions.

Effective corporate governance

Shareholders are a natural force for better corporate performance and profitability. They are the most sensitive to risks among financial players. Foreign investors in particular have led ups and downs in the Japanese stock market, of which the boom triggered by Abenomics in 2013 was only the most recent example. Whenever potential changes in the economy are foreseen, foreign investors are the first to accept the risk and jump in, while Japanese investors duly follow. Some get their fingers burnt when the boom comes to an end.

Japanese investors, generally speaking,

are less willing to demand better performance. In fact, a large share of their investments take the form of bonds, not stock -- that is to say, a stable and predictable but low return, not one at the mercy of market forces but with potentially much greater upside. Considering that corporate profitability has been low for years, one can expect Japanese institutional investors (such as insurance companies or pension funds with long-term perspectives) to urge firms to be more aggressive. But such actions have rarely happened. Activist investors tend to come from abroad, as in the recent case of Sony, where an activist investor proposed that its entertainment business be separately listed in the US. Moreover, Japanese institutional investors are behind their European counterparts in coming up with corporate governance guidelines.

Why this passiveness? Once again, it comes back to practices of employment and career. The investment firms are staffed by life-long employees whose pay are only barely linked to performance. The largest institutional investor in Japan (actually, the largest in the world) is the Government Pension Investment Fund, known as GPIF. Its conservative, risk-averse stance has set the tone for the growth-shy investment landscape of Japan.

A government panel has been established to encourage GPIF to shift towards a more balanced portfolio, by increasing its share of stocks, rather than relying on a mountain of bonds offering low returns. A single change like this could have broad, beneficial repercussions. It could trigger a more general change in the behavior of Japanese fund managers as champions of higher corporate profitability. This, together with more active institutional investors (the FSA in mid 2014 issued a code of responsible practices and encouraged them to sign up), and a recent increase in foreign investment in Japanese companies, helps to raise the pressure on Japanese firms to perform.

Technology start-ups

Improving profitably is a requirement for existing firms, but it says nothing about the need for a broader renewal of the business sector through the creation of new firms altogether. Though it may today seem like a long shot, fostering start-ups that can grow rapidly and ultimately become Japan's leading companies of the future is the key to sustainable growth.

These new firms are likely to be built on the foundation of science and technology. Universities and research institutes both in the public and private sectors are the bedrock of breakthrough ideas and great companies. Of course, Japan's record on scientific and technological research is impressive. It has produced numerous Nobel laureates, along with its many excellent researchers. Measured by indicators such as the level of business investment in R&D relative to GDP, or the number of patents granted, Japan continues to rank high in the international league tables.

However, when it comes to transforming research into full-fledged businesses, Japan has consistently underperformed. The size of venture capital relative to the overall economy is the tiniest among OECD countries. As with other Japanese weaknesses, the low labor mobility is the first culprit. But it is increasingly clear for younger Japanese that even if one has lifetime employment, one's salary grows much slower than those of earlier generations. This fact gives them a little incentive to leave big companies and universities for younger, hungrier businesses.

The idea "cloning" Silicon Valley is not easily achieved. It is hard to identify the right government policies, other than to relax stringent labor rules designed for how the economy existed in the mid 20th century. But at the least, government support and resources should be redirected away from existing companies and towards start-ups. A decision by the Abe administration to increase funding for national, research universities (by about $1 billion), and to support venture capital, are moves in the right direction. But they are just first steps. The policy has been poorly informed by the experience of middling venture practices, and raise concerns over whether the government's budget may be misspent.

Still, if universities and research institutes fully embrace the idea of business incubation, and this is combined with the skills and experiences of the world's best venture funds, then there is a chance that the engines for tomorrow's economic growth will finally have been re-ignited. Prime Minister Abe's arrows will hit their bull's eye, and Japan will be back.

Conclusion

There are reasons for cautious optimism. In a book published in 2011, Professor Yasuyuki Todo of the University of Tokyo analyzed the productivity of many Japanese companies. He found that the average productivity level of "global firms" exposed to international business was higher than that of "non-global firms". At the same time, however, he showed that there were non-global firms whose productivity is much higher still than the average productivity of global firms. These firms exist regardless of sector and size. The findings represent powerful statistical evidence to suggest that there is a large, unexploited source of economic growth in Japan.

The question then becomes: what triggers this growth? In the preceding pages, I have argued that Japan's economic policy agenda has been already been well established and honed. The moment of declaration has turned into the moment for implementation. Politicians and bureaucrats must now actually make the necessary reforms; put the ideas in practice. Yet the more comprehensive the reforms, the more they threaten the interests of incumbent players, be it those of big business or bureaucrats. They entail difficulties in engaging and persuading vested interests about the larger gains at stake, economy-wide, and for the long-term survival of the country. Politicians and bureaucrats must face up to the challenge; Japan's leaders must truly lead.

To be sure, the broad range and depth of Japan's problems push some observers to conclude that it is unrealistic to expect a path of vigorous economic growth. But there are stronger reasons to embrace optimism.

First is historical precedent. Looking back at Japan in late 19th century, the Tokugawa government returned power to the Emperor in 1868, an epic event. But even after that, Japan consisted of about 300 self-autarkic local blocs (called *Han*), each of which was ruled by a hereditary feudal lord and other traditional elites.

The new administration, largely made up of middle class samurai, could not implement modernization policies that were critically needed.

Yet their leaders never gave up. After a relentless and determined effort, they succeeded in 1871 in replacing *Han* with the modern regional unit of *Ken*, making it possible for Japan to become a unified state with a common monetary, fiscal and legal structure. Without the 1871 reforms, the Meiji Revolution and the modernization of Japan would have ended just on paper, not in practice.

In other words, Japan has in its heritage a potent example of endogenous and fundamental reform, so long as the sense of crisis is broadly shared. (Whether this idea of common pain and potential gain exists, however, is an important element missing in the current policy discussions.)

Second, is the role of expectations in the private sector. Economic growth comes from companies and consumers. Their actions depend on what they expect of the future. Well in advance, before all the necessary reforms are actually implemented, private sector actors will invest -- so long as they are reasonably certain that the promised changes will come.

One example is the experience of the Koizumi Cabinet in 2001 to 2006. Although it is generally considered to be a period of radical change, the achievements were extremely uneven. Yes, much fiscal progress occurred by imposing budgetary controls, non-performing bank loans were greatly reduced, and the privatization of postal services was agreed after heated political disputes. At the same time, however, in areas like regulatory reform, nothing notable happened. Still, the economy regained momentum from almost zero GDP growth in 2001 to about 1.8% on average between 2003 and 2007.

This shows that firms, although aware that progress was patchy, still believed that reforms would continue and the scope of business would further expand. So they increased investment, which fueled growth. And the actual economic improvement confirmed corporate expectations, which in turn made businesses more optimistic. This virtuous cycle was seen to work. Comprehensive reforms are indispensable for Japan, but all of them do not have to be carried out at once, immediately.

Can Japan bounce back? So far in the 21th century, Japanese share prices measured by the year-end level of the Nikkei Stock Average was the highest for 2006 at ¥17200, an achievement of the Koizumi reforms. And after having sunk to their lowest leave, ¥8500 in 2011, they have risen again, reaching ¥16300 in 2013. What the numbers suggest is that we are at a new turning point. A lot depends on psychological factors.

Whether Japan has the capacity to follow through, whether people can trust it, is crucial. Those at the highest positions in government, the bureaucracy and business should defy the naysayers and embrace the long-term vision of reform that can help Japan bounce back. Without the third arrow, the other arrows will not be firm enough: all will be broken. But taken together, the reforms will usher in a new, strong Japan.

www.ingramcontent.com/pod-product-compliance
Lightning Source LLC
Chambersburg PA
CBHW032017190326
41520CB00007B/514